Edward's Invitations

1885 - 1887

compiled by

Diane Janowski

Edward's Invitations
compiled by Diane Janowski

Published by New York History Review Press, Elmira, New York

For the latest on New York History Review, please visit
www.NewYorkHistoryReview.com

First Edition
ISBN: 978-0-9965353-2-8

Printed and bound in the United States of America.

For Mary Welles

The Victorian era

was a time of refined sensibilities. Parties and social gatherings provided opportunities to display one's status and refinement. Central New York State was no exception.

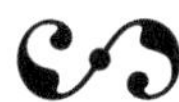

Edward M. Sayre

The Sayre family was among the pioneer settlers of Chemung County. Edward's father Willis B. was a son of Mathew Sayre, who with his brothers, his father, James Sayre, and uncles, came to the Chemung valley from Orange county during the last decade of the eighteenth century.

The Sayre family acquired 800-acres of land in Horseheads, New York. This included a large part of the present village of Horseheads. The Sayres were substantial citizens. Willis B. was born October 2, 1817, in Horseheads. On January 11, 1843, he married Annis H. Fitch. Edward was one of their five children.

At the time of the invitations in these book, 1885 - 1887, Edward was listed in the Elmira City Directory as being a traveling salesman who resided at the Wyckoff House at 115 - 123 West Water Street. He may have at some time during this three-year period, lived with, or worked with Clarence Ferguson, as Clarence received mail for him.

Edward was young, single, and very popular.

February 1885

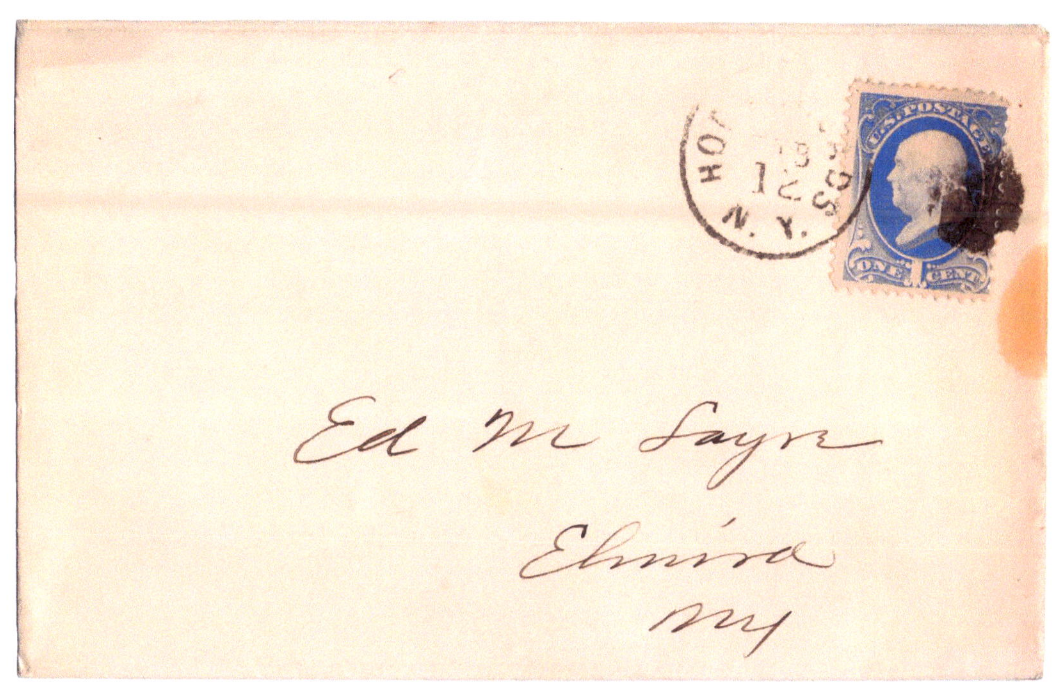

U.S. POSTAGE
ONE CENT
N. Y.
Ed M Sayre
Elmira
NY

Horseheads was sometimes called North Elmira. Pritchard Hall still stands at 117-119 W. Franklin Street.

Reception Committee.

LEVI RELYEA,

C. CARPENTER,

L. C. WHITAKER.

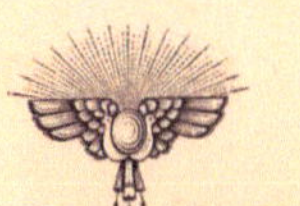

Yourself and Ladies are cordially invited to attend a

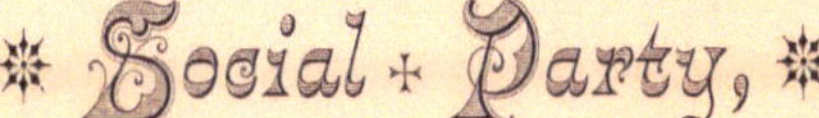

GIVEN BY THE YOUNG GENTLEMEN AT

PRICHARD HALL, NORTH ELMIRA, N. Y.,

Friday Evening, February 19th, 1886.

MUSIC BY CASADY'S FULL ORCHESTRA.

Dancing Bill, $1.00. Grand March at 8:30 Sharp.

This Invitation must be presented at the Door.

Floor Committee.

G. H. BEARD,

A. TERRY,

C. CARPENTER,

L. C. WHITAKER.

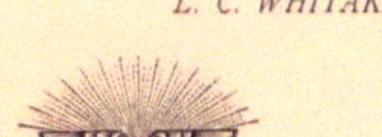

November 1885

ELMIRA
NOV
5 PM
1880
N.Y.

Ed Sayre
Elmira

C/o Weaver + Ferguson

Thanksgiving Party.

Mr. Ed. Sayre

Yourself and lady are respectfully invited to attend a Thanks-giving Party by Chemung Valley Grange, at Farmers' Club Hall,

Thursday Evening, Nov. 26th, '85.

Music by Casady's Orchestra.

Dancing and Supper $1.00; or Supper 50 Cents.

☞PRESENT THIS TICKET AT THE DOOR.

January 1886

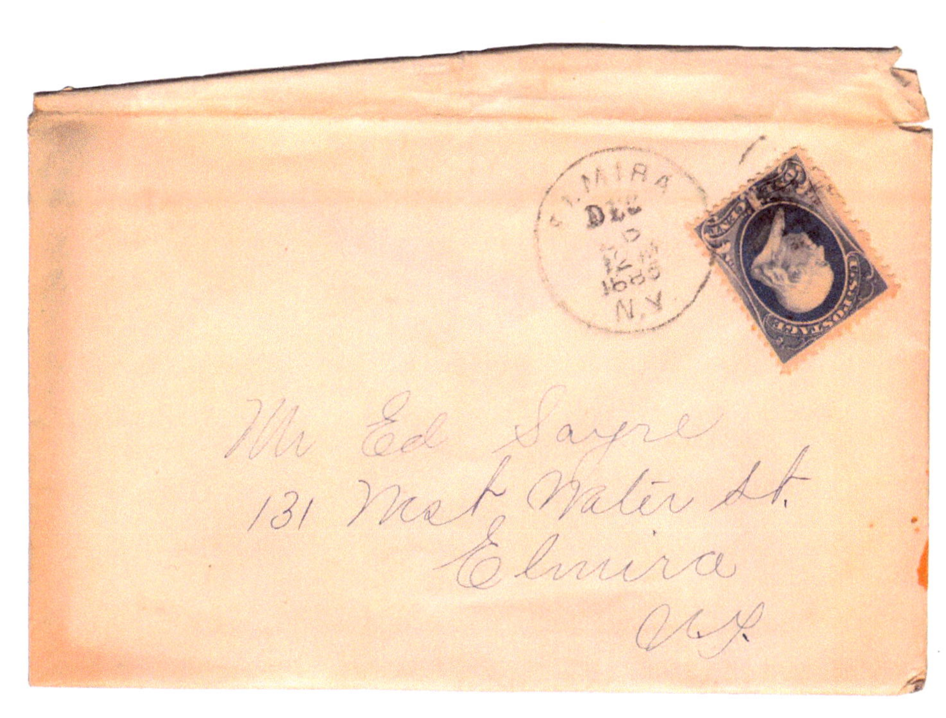
ELMIRA
DEC
N.Y.
Mr Ed Sayre
131 West Water St.
Elmira
N.Y.

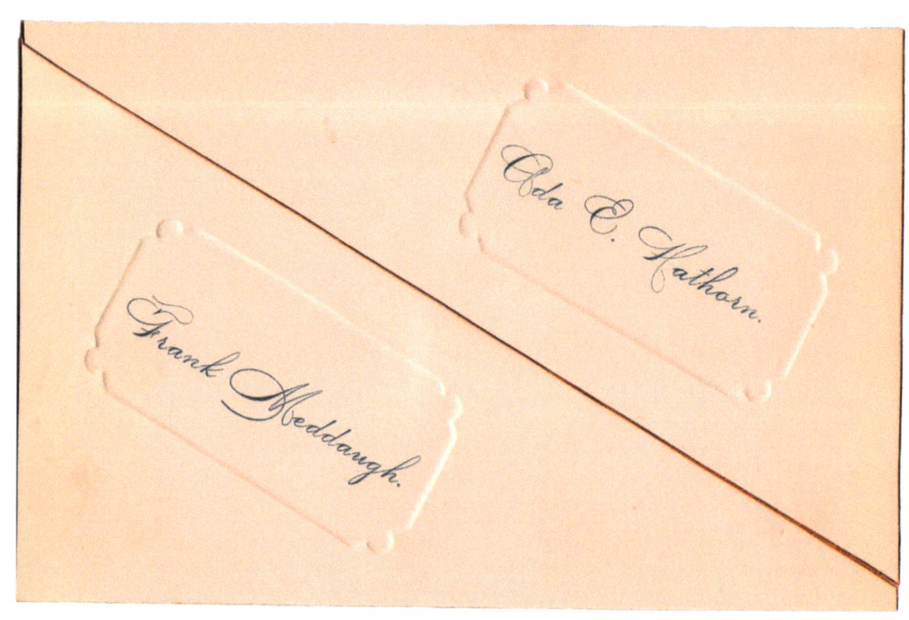
Ada E. Hathorn.
Frank Meddaugh.

Mr. and Mrs. John W. Hathorn
request your presence at the marriage of
their daughter,
Thursday Evening, January 7, 1886.
Ceremony at seven o'clock.
1333 College Avenue, Elmira, N.Y.

January 1886

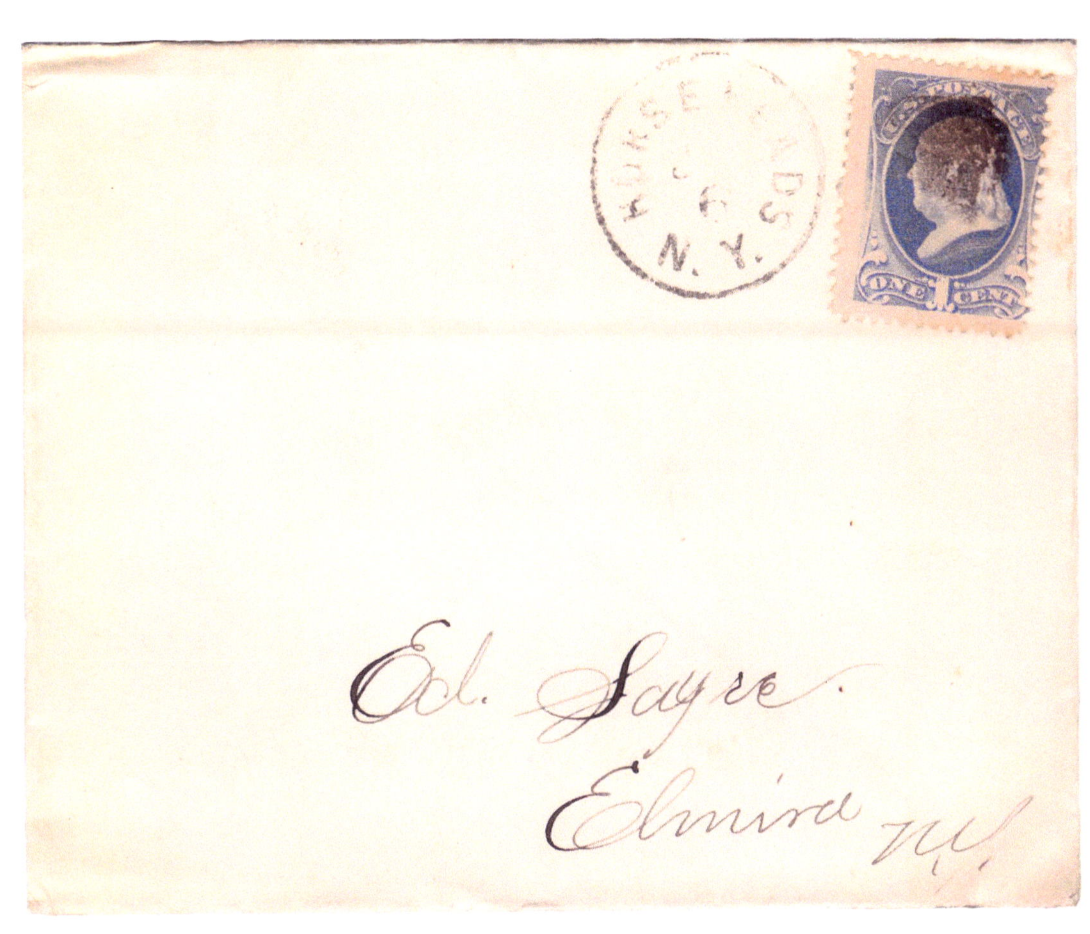
HORSEHEADS
6
N.Y.
U.S. POSTAGE
ONE CENT
Ed. Sayre
Elmira N.Y.

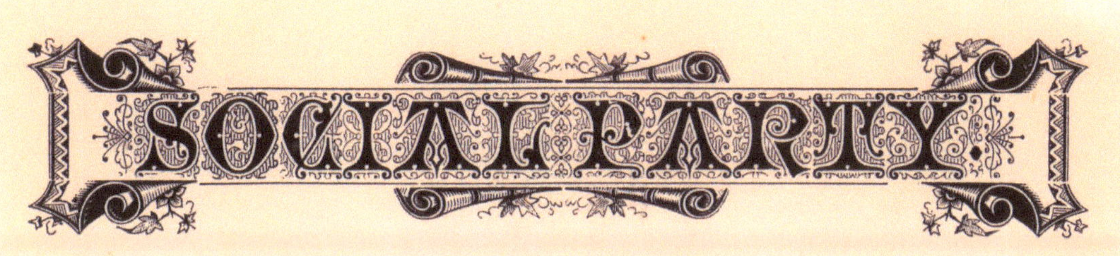

Yourself and Ladies are cordially invited to attend a Social Party, given by the Young Men of Horseheads, at

WHITCOMB HALL

Friday Evening, January 15th, 1886.

DANCE TICKET, 75 CTS. SUPPER, 50 CTS.

MUSIC, CASSADY'S FULL ORCHESTRA, OF ELMIRA.

PLEASE PRESENT THIS CARD AT THE DOOR.

February 1886

Clarence Ferguson was a salesman who lived at 133 West Water Street.

ELMIRA
FEB 17
12 30 PM
86

U.S. POSTAGE
ONE CENT

Ed. Sayre
Care Ferguson
Elmira

Grange Reception.

Yourself and Ladies are respectfully invited to attend
a Reception, to be given by

Chemung Valley Grange,

NO. 57.

At Farmers' Club Hall, Elmira, N. Y., on

Thursday Evening, February 25th, '86.

MUSIC BY CASSIDY'S ORCHESTRA.

BILL, including Supper, $1.00. Supper 50 cents. Ladies free. NOT TRANSFERABLE.

March 1886

Mr. Ed Sayre
Elmira
N.Y.

CLOSING RECEPTION

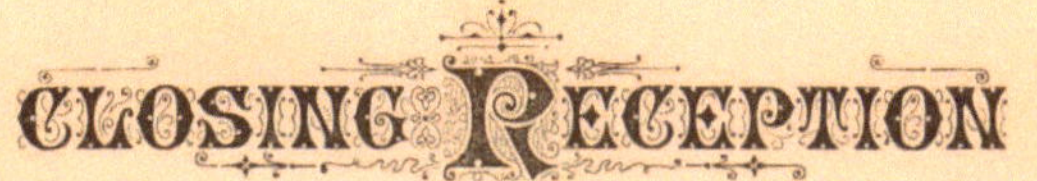

I. S. CLUB.

Yourself and ladies are cordially invited to attend the closing reception of this season, at

LOWMAN'S HALL, WELLSBURG.

Friday Evening, March 5th, 1886.

RECEPTION COMMITTEE.	FLOOR MANAGERS.
A. G. MILLER.	G. P. MCHENRY.
E. M. LEVERICH.	TIM MATTHEWS.
MARTIN LOWMAN.	C. E. VANBUSKIRK.

Dance Tickets, 50c. **Supper Tickets, 50c.**

MUSIC--CASADY'S FULL ORCHESTRA.

This Invitation must be shown at the door.

April 1886

Mr. Ed Sayre
Elmira
N.Y.

I. S. CLUB RECEPTION

Yourself and ladies are cordially invited to attend a reception to be held at

LOWMAN'S HALL, WELLSBURG

Friday Evening, April 30th, 1886.

RECEPTION COMMITTEE.

A. G. MILLER,
E. M. LEVERICH,
MARTIN LOWMAN.

FLOOR MANAGERS.

G. P. MCHENRY.
TIM MATTHEWS.
C. E. VANBUSKIRK,

Dance Tickets, 50c. **Supper Tickets, 50c.**

MUSIC--CASADY'S FULL ORCHESTRA.

This Invitation must be shown at the door.

June 1886

This invitation had no envelope.

Strawberry & Ice Cream Party,

—BY—

Chemung Valley Grange,

At Farmers' Club Hall, Elmira, N. Y.

FRIDAY EVENING, JUNE 18, 1886.

YOURSELF AND LADIES ARE INVITED.

Dancing and Supper Tickets, $1.00. Supper Tickets without privilege of Dancing, 50 cents.

This Invitation not Transferable. ***Casady's Orchestra.***

GENERAL COMMITTEE.

Albert Simmons,	M. H. Thurston,	Hattie McCann,	Crete McCann,
Elmer Baldwin,	Geo. E. Harris,	Mamie Ford,	Addie Jenkins.

August 1886

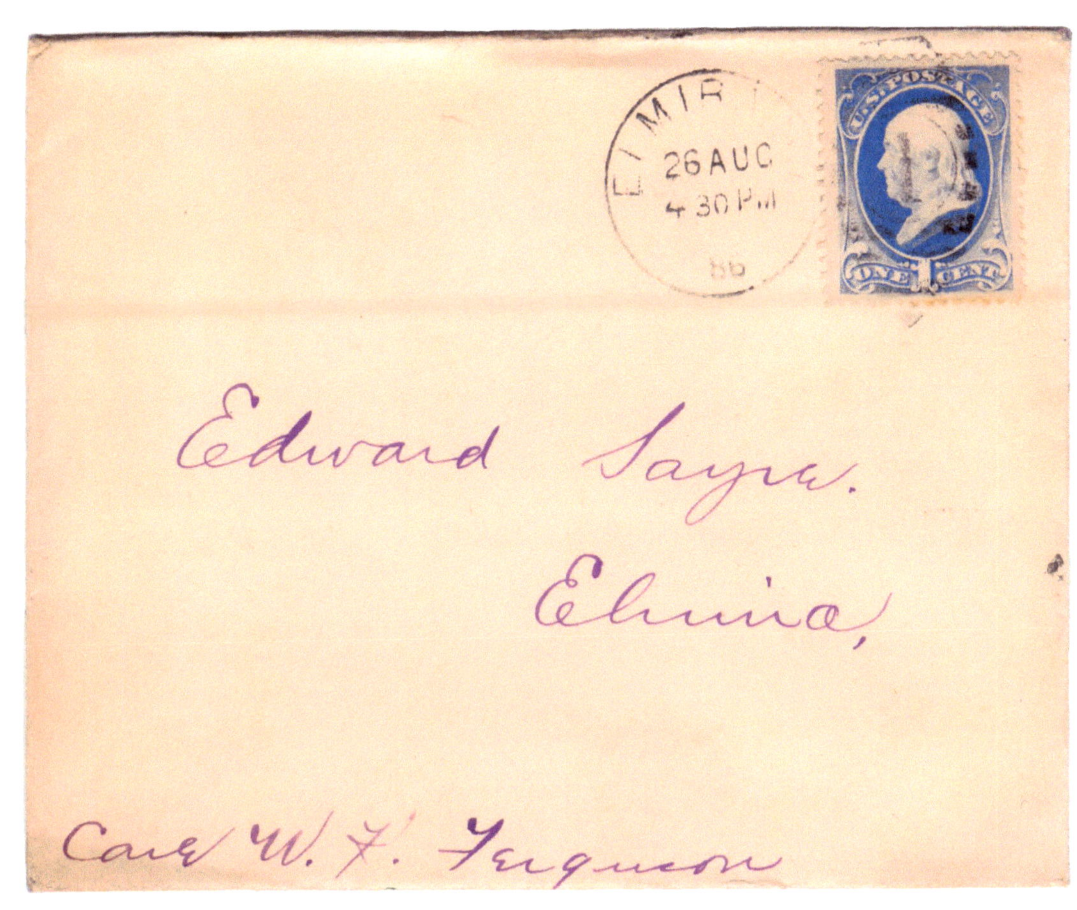
MIR
26 AUG
4 30 PM
86
U.S. POSTAGE
ONE CENT
Edward Sayre.
Elmira,
Care W. F. Ferguson

The F. I. Club,

RESPECTFULLY INVITE YOURSELF AND LADIES TO ATTEND THEIR FIRST HOP,

Tuesday Evening, August 31st, 1886,

AT FARMERS' CLUB HALL, ELMIRA, N. Y.

—COMMITTEE.—

M. B. HELLER. J. D. McCANN.

MUSIC BY CASSIDY'S ORCHESTRA.

Bill, $1.25. Dancing commences at 8:30.

September 1886

Mr. Ed Sayre
Elmira
N.Y.

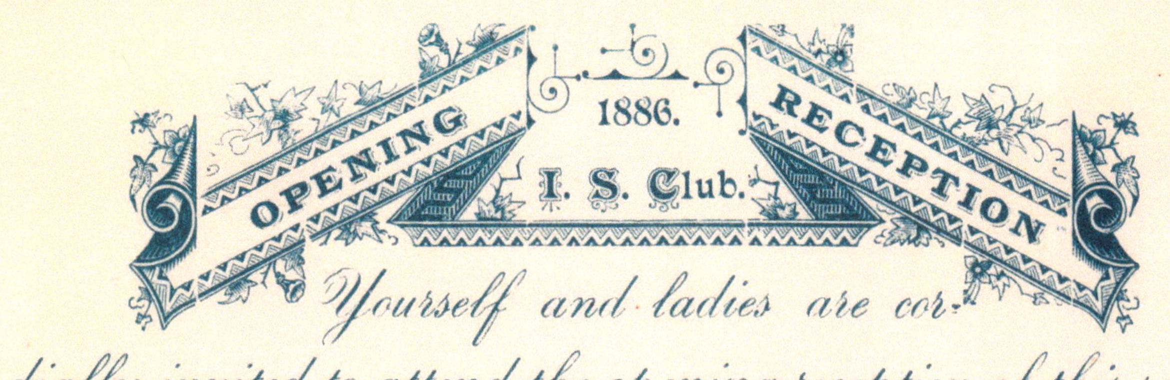

Yourself and ladies are cordially invited to attend the opening reception of this season

AT

LOWMAN'S HALL, WELLSBURG,

Friday Evening, September 3d, 1886.

RECEPTION COMMITTEE.	FLOOR MANAGERS.
A. G. MILLER,	G. P. MCHENRY,
E. M. LEVERICH,	TIM MATTHEWS,
MARTIN LOWMAN.	C. E. VANBUSKIRK.

Dancing Tickets, 50c. **Supper Tickets. 50c.**

Music--Casady's Full Orchestra,

This Invitation must be shown at the door.

October 1886

ELMIRA
OCT
21
5 PM
1885
N.Y.

ELMIRA
OCT
5 PM
1885
N.Y.

U.S. POSTAGE
ONE CENT

Ed Sayre
Elmira

The Chemung County Grange #57 met monthly every second Saturday at the Farmer's Club Hall on Hoffman Street near West Hill Road.

Grange Reception.

Yourself and Ladies are respectfully invited to attend a Reception to be given by Chemung Valley Grange, No. 57, at Farmers' Club Hall, Elmira, N. Y., on

Friday Evening, October 30th, '85.

MUSIC BY CASSIDY'S ORCHESTRA.

Bill, including Supper $1.00, Supper 50 cents. Ladies free. NOT TRANSFERABLE.

December 1886

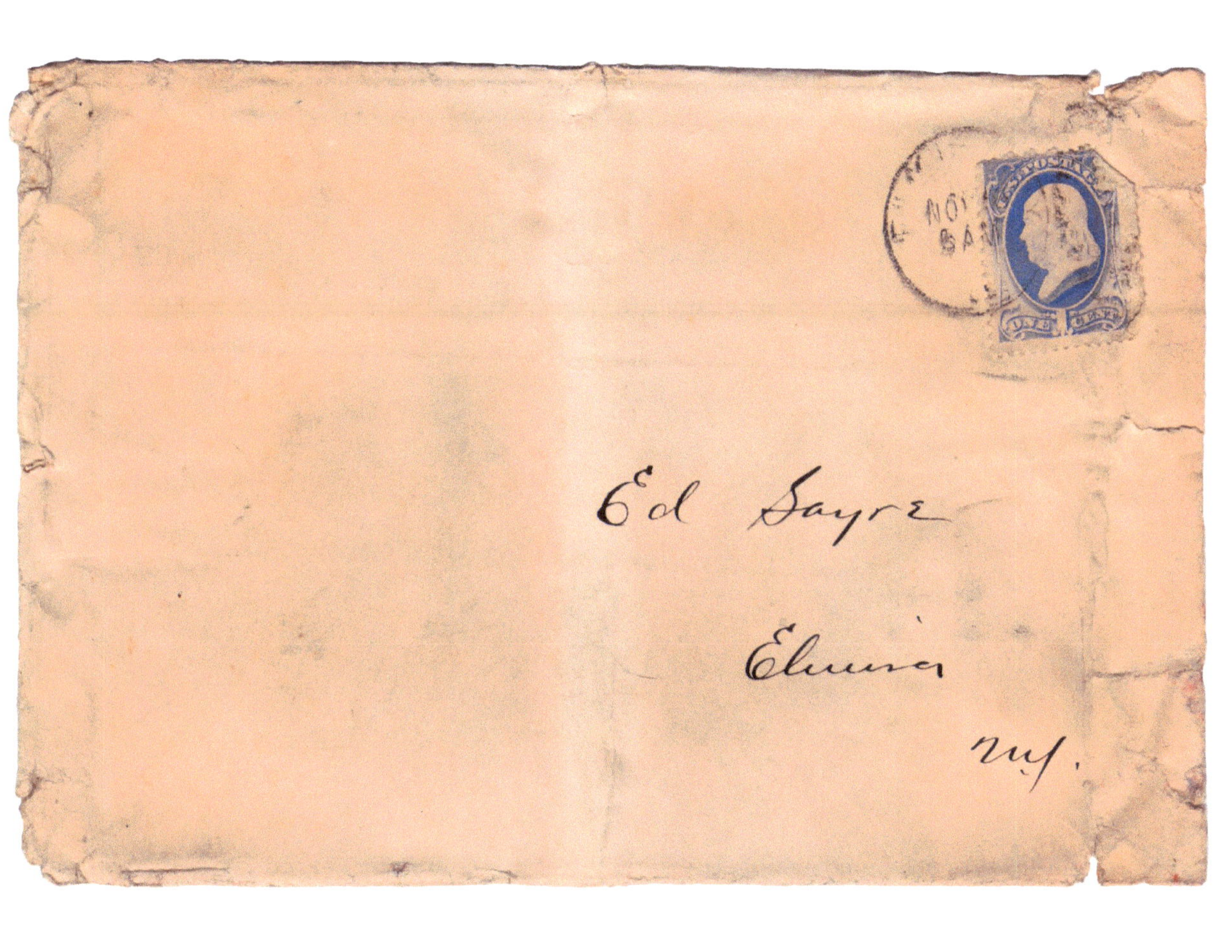
Ed Sayre
Elmira
N.Y.

St. Omers' Commandery was a Masonic organization that regularly met the first and third Fridays of every month at the Masonic Temple on the corner of Lake and Market Streets in Elmira.

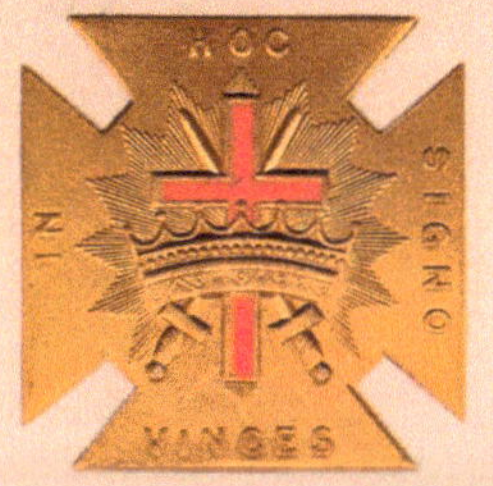

Elmira, Nov. 15, 1886.

The Pleasure of Your Company with Ladies is Requested by

St. Omers' Commandery,

No. 19, K. T.,

to attend their Annual Receptions, Season of 1886-7,

Masonic Temple.

Thanksgiving Night, Nov. 25,

Friday Eve'gs, Dec. 10, 31, '86. Jan. 14, 28 and Feb. 11, '87.

MUSIC FURNISHED BY DRISCOLL & FLEMMING'S FULL ORCHESTRA.

Reception Committee.

John B. Stanchfield, E. C.
L. M. Millspaugh, S. B.
Herbert Johnson.

Jno. T. Hill, Geno.
Levi D. Little,
Robt. A. Walker.

December 1886

This invitation is addressed to Mr. Ferguson.

U.S. POSTAGE
ONE CENT

WELLS[illegible]
N. Y.

Mr. C. H. Furguson
Elmira
N.Y.

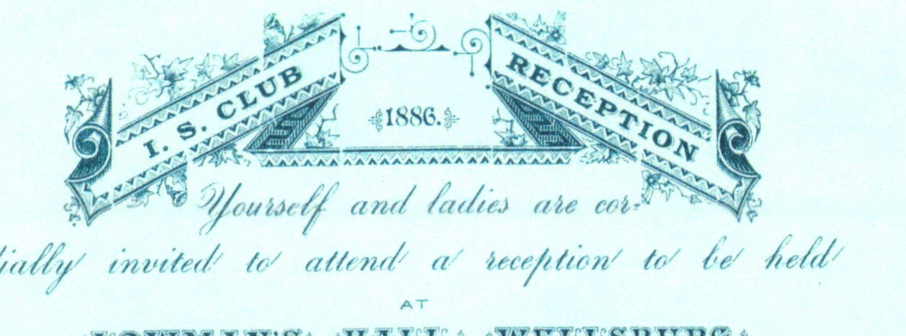

Yourself and ladies are cordially invited to attend a reception to be held

AT

LOWMAN'S HALL, WELLSBURG,

Friday Evening, December 10th, 1886.

RECEPTION COMMITTEE.	FLOOR MANAGERS.
A. G. MILLER,	G. P. MCHENRY,
E. M. LEVERICH,	TIM MATTHEWS,
MARTIN LOWMAN.	C. E. VANBUSKIRK.

Dancing Tickets, 50c. **Supper Tickets. 50c.**

Music--Pine's Full Orchestra,

This Invitation must be shown at the door. Dancing will begin at 8 o'clock.

December 1886

Mr. Ed. Sayre
Elmira
N.Y.

M Ed. Sayre

Yourself and Ladies are cordially invited to attend a Social Hop at Lowman's Hall, Wellsburg,

Thursday Eve. Dec. 31

Under the auspices of the I. S. Club.

FLOOR MANAGERS.

A. G. MILLER,	MARTIN LOWMAN,	E. M. LEVERICH,
C. E. VANBUSKIRK,	GUY MCHENRY,	TIM MATHEWS.

Music--Pines' Orchestra. Bill--50 Cents.

Present this at the door.

January 1887

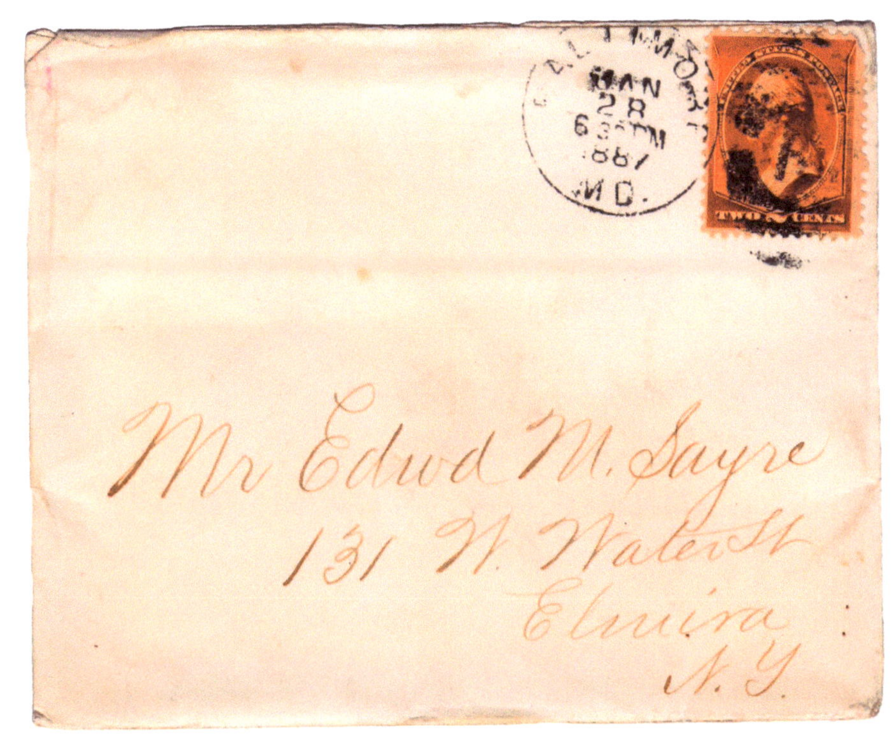

JAN
28
MD.
TWO CENTS
Mr Edwd M. Sayre
131 N. Water St
Elmira
N.Y.

Mr. & Mrs. William P. Blades

announce the marriage of their daughter,

Sara May,

to

Mr. Edward B. Billings,

on Tuesday, January twenty-fifth,

eighteen hundred and eighty-seven,

Grace Church,

Baltimore.

Mr. Edward M. Sayre.

Mr. & Mrs. Edward B. Billings.

At Home,
after February eighth.

352 West Clinton Street,
Elmira, N.Y.

More from New York History Review

Victorian Pride - Forgotten Songs of Central New York 1841-1885

Victorian Pride - Forgotten Songs of Upstate New York 1850 - 1884

Victorian Pride - Forgotten Songs of Pennsylvania

Victorian Pride - Forgotten Songs of America

Victorian Pride - Victorian Wedding Songs

The Great Inter-State Fair, Elmira, New York 1890

Please visit our websites

www.NewYorkHistoryReview.com

www.VictorianPride.com

www.ingramcontent.com/pod-product-compliance
Lightning Source LLC
LaVergne TN
LVHW070144110826
845147LV00002B/321
9780996535328